THE APACHES AND NAVAJOS

CRAIG A. DOHERTY AND KATHERINE M. DOHERTY

THE APACHES AND NAVAJOS

Franklin Watts   New York   London   Toronto   Sydney   A First Book

First Paperback Edition 1991

Map by Joe Le Monnier / Cover photograph courtesy of: Michal Heron

Photographs courtesy of: American Museum of Natural History: p. 3;
Museum of the American Indian: p. 15; Museum für Volkerkunde, Berlin:
p. 18; The Stock Market: p. 19 (Marcia Keegan); Photo Researchers: p. 20
(Tom McHugh/Indian City, USA); Marcia Keegan: pp. 25, 39, 43 (top);
Michal Heron: pp. 26, 27 (top), 32, 35 (both), 59; Utah State Histori-
cal Society: pp. 27 (bottom), 30; Denver Art Museum: p. 33 (H. Begay);
Denver Museum of Natural History: p. 43 (bottom); Arizona Historical
Society: p. 48 (top); Jerry Jacka: pp. 48 (bottom), 50, 54, 57 (left), 61
(bottom); Art Resource: p. 51 (Joseph Martin/Scala); Granger Collec-
tion: p. 57 (right); Paul Conkin: p. 61 (top).

Library of Congress Cataloging-in-Publication Data
Doherty, Craig A.
The Apaches and Navajos / by Craig A. Doherty and Katherine M. Doherty.
p. cm.—(A First book)
Bibliography: p.
Includes index.
Summary: Discusses the traditional daily life of the Apaches and Navajos.
ISBN 0-531-10743-4 (lib.)/ISBN 0-531-15602-8 (pbk.)
1. Apache Indians—Juvenile literature.   2. Navajo Indians—Juvenile
literature.   [1. Apache Indians.   2. Navajo Indians.   3. Indians of
North America.]   I. Doherty, Katherine M.   II. Title.   III. Series.
E99.A6D64   1989
973'.04972—dc20   89-9079   CIP   AC

CONTENTS

THE APACHES AND NAVAJOS

INTRODUCTION

Most scientists believe that the Indians of the Americas originally came from Asia. They were hunters of big game—woolly mammoths and bison. The hunters could have arrived during the last Ice Age, fifteen to forty thousand years ago. As more and more of the world's moisture turned to ice and became part of the glaciers of the Ice Age, the oceans receded, exposing more land. The shallow Bering Sea, between Asia and North America, became a land bridge that allowed the nomadic Asians to migrate to North America. Once they had crossed the land bridge, they eventually spread out and inhabited all of North, South, and Central America.

In time, the glaciers receded and the world began to warm up. The big-game hunters had to adapt to new environments in the various parts of the Americas where they lived. Where game and wild edible plants were plentiful, Indians remained nomadic (wandered). Other Indians learned how to cultivate plants for food and settled in permanent communities. Some regions, where the soil and climate were good and the game plentiful, were home to both hunter-nomads and farmers. There were many different Indian groups in the Americas when the Europeans began arriving, in the late fifteenth century.

APACHE AND NAVAJO PREHISTORY

The southwestern part of the United States contains many different Indian groups. The various Pueblo groups were farmers. The Athapaskan tribes, the Navajos and Apaches, were nomads. The Athapaskans migrated to the Southwest from northern Canada.

They left the north about a thousand years ago, possibly because of famine, and migrated south along the Rocky Mountains. As they traveled south, they adapted to their new surroundings.

The Athapaskans may have arrived in the Southwest around the year 1300. The Athapaskans may have first learned agriculture and how to make pottery from the existing Pueblos.

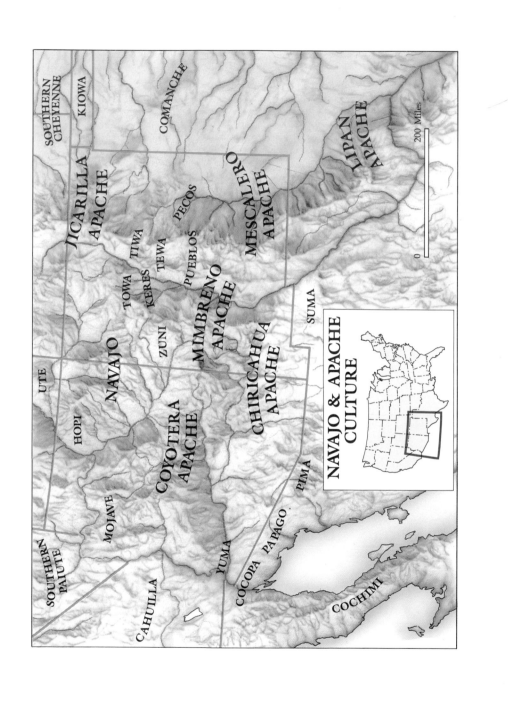

NAVAJO & APACHE CULTURE

When the Spanish began to arrive in the 1500s, they called the southwestern Athapaskan people "Apaches." The word Apache is believed to be derived from the Zuni Puebloan word for enemy. The Spanish named the groups based on where they lived or what they did. The Spanish names were Apache de Jicarilla, those who wove baskets that could be used as water containers; Apache de Mescalero, those who ate mescal; Apache de Navajo, those who cultivated fields; Apache de Gila, those who lived in the Gila Mountain region.

The Apachean people share the source of their language with other groups. Among the Apachean people, there are seven different Athapaskan languages: Navajo, Western Apache, Chiricahua, Mescalero, Jicarilla, Lipan, and Kiowa-Apache. And the Apachean people who speak each language are considered a separate group and are called by the name of their language—Navajos, Western Apaches, and so on.

THE COMING OF THE EUROPEANS

The Apachean people learned many things from the Puebloan groups. But it was the coming of the Spanish that had the biggest influence on the Apaches and Navajos. By 1680 the Spanish had established communities all along the Rio Grande River in what is now New Mexico. In that year the Rio Grande Pueblos banded together and drove the Spanish back to Mexico. This is called the Pueblo Revolt. When the Spanish reconquered New Mexico, many Puebloans fled to live among the Navajos. The Puebloans living among the Navajos taught them many things from their own culture and from the Spanish culture.

From the Spanish, the Apachean people acquired horses, sheep, and other animals. The horse gave the

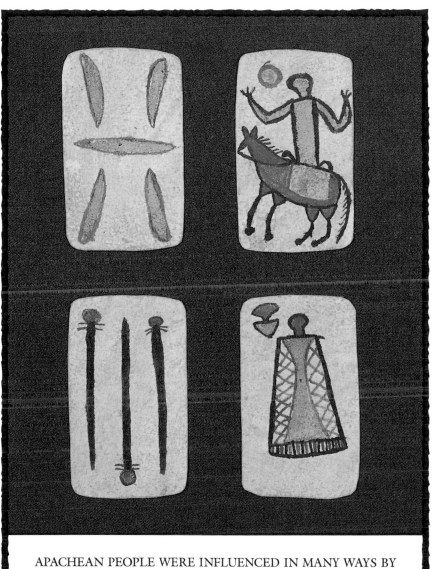

APACHEAN PEOPLE WERE INFLUENCED IN MANY WAYS BY
THE SPANISH. THESE RAWHIDE CARDS, FOR EXAMPLE,
ARE AN IMITATION OF SPANISH PLAYING CARDS.

Apachean people great mobility. They could now travel quickly from one place to another. The Apachean people also learned other things from the Spanish. They learned how to use wool in their weaving and to make jewelry out of silver. These crafts are still very important, especially to the Navajos.

After the Mexican-American War, the Southwest became part of the United States. The U.S. government spent many years fighting against the Apachean people. In 1865 the U.S. Army defeated the Navajos, and over nine thousand Navajos were sent as prisoners to Fort Sumner, New Mexico, 300 miles (500 km) away. Many died on the way to Fort Sumner, and many more while being held there. In 1868 the Navajos who remained were allowed to return to their homeland in the Four Corners area. The Four Corners is the place where Arizona, New Mexico, Utah, and Colorado come together. The Navajo called this event the Long Walk and still teach their children about this terrible experience.

At different times almost all of the Apache tribes fought against the U.S. Army. Eventually the Apaches were all defeated and forced to settle on reservations set up by the U.S. government.

Today most Apaches and Navajos still live on these reservations. There are two Apache reservations in Arizona and two Apache reservations in New Mexico.

SOCIAL ORGANIZATION

The Apachean peoples are divided into two major groups: the Navajos and the Apaches. The Navajos are the largest American Indian group in the United States. They consider themselves members of one nation. The Apaches are divided into six different tribes. The six tribes were split geographically by the Rio Grande River in New Mexico. The Mescalero, Jicarilla, Lipan, and Kiowa Apaches lived east of the Rio Grande. The Western Apaches and the Chiricahuas lived west of the river.

The four Apache tribes that lived east of the Rio Grande were influenced by the Plains Indians who were to their east.

The Mescalero Apaches ranged over southeastern

THE NAVAJOS WERE ONE OF THE TWO MAJOR
GROUPS OF THE APACHEAN PEOPLES. THE
STRIPED BLANKETS SHOWN IN THIS PAINTING
OF NAVAJOS GAVE WAY IN THE 1890S
TO BLANKETS WITH INTRICATE PATTERNS,
FAVORED BY WHITE BUYERS.

New Mexico and into west Texas and northern Mexico. Today the Mescalero Apaches live on the Mescalero Reservation in south-central New Mexico. They share this reservation with the Chiricahua and Lipan Apache tribes.

The Jicarilla Apaches arrived in the Southwest later than some of the other Apachean groups. The Jicarillas inhabited the Southern end of the Rocky Mountains and part of the plains of southeastern Colorado. Today they live on the Jicarilla Apache Reservation in north-central New Mexico. The Lipan Apaches roamed the southeastern plains of Colorado and part of northern New Mexico. Today they live on the Mescalero Apache Reservation in central New Mexico. The Kiowa Apaches are a small group that allied themselves with the Kiowa Indians in Oklahoma. The Kiowa are a Plains Indian group. The Kiowa Apaches still live among the Kiowas in Oklahoma.

A KIOWA
IN COLORFUL
HEADDRESS.

[19]

THIS IS A RECONSTRUCTION OF
A CHIRICAHUA APACHE LODGE.

West of the Rio Grande, the Chiricahua Apaches were divided into three main bands. The Eastern Chiricahuas, also called the Red Paint People, ranged over southwestern New Mexico. The Central Chiricahuas inhabited eastern Arizona and northern Mexico. The Southern Chiricahuas occupied lands mostly in Mexico as well as in southwestern New Mexico. The Southern Chiricahuas called themselves the Enemy People.

The Western Apaches lived in eastern Arizona and were divided into four groups. These groups are the

[20]

White Mountain Apaches, the San Carlos Apaches, the Cibecue Apaches, and the Tonto Apaches. Today the Western Apaches live on the San Carlos and Fort Apache reservations in Arizona.

Bands, Clans, and Outfits → Apache tribes were organized into smaller groups called bands. A band was made up of a number of local groups that all camped in the same general area. The local groups would be made up of people who camped together and often shared the work. Within the local group, there would be a few different extended families. An extended family usually consisted of a grandmother and her husband, her daughters and their husbands, and all their children. Each local group had its own leader and was independent.

The Apache families were matrilineal. This means they followed the mother's side of the family. When a daughter of the family married, she and her husband would stay with her mother's group. When a son married, he would go to live with his wife's family.

The fact that the groups and bands were only loosely associated with each other made it hard for the U.S. government to reach agreements with the Apache people. The government would make a treaty with one band and would incorrectly assume they had made a treaty with all the Apaches.

The Navajos followed the same matrilineal rules as the other Apachean tribes but organized the families more formally into clans. There are over sixty Navajo clans. Each Navajo child is a member of his or her mother's clan. The child's father would belong to a different clan. A Navajo who is ready for marriage must choose someone who is not a member of either his or her mother's or father's clan.

Often two or more extended families would get together to help each other. This might include help with planting or harvesting. It might include moving the herds and flocks from winter to summer range. When families worked together like this, they were called an outfit.

Among the Navajos, the family is very important. Large families stay together. These families have a head mother and often share a large flock of sheep and an area of range land where their sheep graze. Unlike the other Apachean groups, the Navajos sometimes live with the husband's family, although it is more common to find young couples moving in with the wife's family.

RELIGION AND BELIEFS

Every culture has its own version of how life originated. Many Americans believe the creation story presented in the Bible. The Apaches and Navajos have their own versions of how they came to exist.

Most Apaches and Navajos believe that the first man and woman of their tribe came up from under the surface of the earth. The first man and woman brought with them the ceremonies the people would need. In the different versions of the story, it is a long and hard journey. Many obstacles had to be overcome before the couple reached the surface. Some spirits helped them; others tried to harm them. All these spirits are still part of the beliefs of many Apaches and Navajos. The description of this journey is one of the first things children are taught about their culture.

Among the Apaches and Navajos it is almost impossible to separate their religion from their everyday life. Everything they do is somehow connected with or affected by their religious beliefs. A successful hunt depends on following the proper rituals and the guidance of the spirits of the hunt. Blessings are sought when new homes are built.

Everything has its place in the universe of the Apaches and Navajos. Many of their ceremonies are intended to insure that the proper order is maintained. The Apaches and Navajos recognize that there is both good and evil in the world. They also know that there is good and evil within each person. They believe that when a person dies, the evil within becomes a dangerous ghost. They have rituals that are aimed at controlling these ghosts.

One of the most important of the Navajo ceremonies is the healing sing. To cure someone of an apparent sickness, that person becomes the center of a healing sing. For each type of sickness there is a sand painting (or dry painting), an appropriate chant, and herbal medicines.

The healing sing is centered around the creation of the appropriate sand painting. Sand paintings are generally done on the floor of the hogan (log struc-

RELIGION HAS ALWAYS BEEN EXTREMELY IMPORTANT
TO THE APACHES AND NAVAJOS. THIS NAVAJO GIRL
SCATTERS CORNMEAL AS A PRAYER AT SUNRISE.

ture). There are many different sand painting designs. Each design is supposed to have the power to cure a certain ailment. Each sand painting depicts the masked supernatural beings that are being called on to help cure the patient.

The sand paintings vary greatly in size. Some are as small as 1 foot (0.3 m) square. Others are as big as 20 feet (6.1 m) across. The top of the sand painting always faces east, the direction the gods are believed to come from. The sand painting is usually done in the hogan of the person being treated. The medicine man, or Hataalii, and his helpers create the sand painting using a variety of substances.

RIGHT AND FACING PAGE: A SIGNIFICANT NAVAJO CEREMONY IS THE HEALING SING. ACCOMPANYING EACH HEALING SING IS A SAND PAINTING THAT DEPICTS THE SUPER-NATURAL BEINGS CALLED ON TO HELP THE PATIENT.

BELOW: A NAVAJO MEDICINE MAN.

The most used materials in sand paintings are various colored sands. When additional colors are needed, other substances—such as charcoal, cornmeal, pollen, and colored rocks—are finely ground and used.

For a daytime healing, the sand painting is begun early in the morning, and the ceremony is performed. Then the sand painting is destroyed before sunset. For a nighttime healing, the sand painting is begun after sunset and destroyed before sunrise.

After the sand painting is completed, the person being treated sits on the painting and the ceremony continues. Healing songs are sung, aromatic herbs are burned, and herbal medicines are administered.

In some instances the healing process includes masked dancers, who represent the supernatural beings depicted in the sand paintings. Their dancing gives more power to the healing process.

Another strong belief among the Apaches and Navajos is the belief in shamans. A shaman is usually a person who is believed to be in contact with the elements of power in the world. Some shamans use their power in evil ways; others use it to help people.

Geronimo, a great Apache war chief, was considered to be a very powerful shaman. He used his power to foresee the outcome of battles. Shamans could also aid in curing people, help insure successful hunts, and act as go-betweens with the supernatural powers.

DAILY LIFE

Daily life among the Apachean people has changed over the centuries. Today many of the Navajos and Apaches live lives that are not that much different from their non-Indian neighbors. However, there are many Navajos and Apaches who live a more "traditional" lifestyle.

When the Apachean people first came to the Southwest, they were hunters and gatherers. They moved systematically around their area. Even today, many Navajos move from winter grazing lands to summer ranges.

Infancy ➤ At birth, Apache and Navajo babies were placed in cradleboards. Many Apache and Navajo

AS WITH MANY OTHER INDIAN NATIONS, THE
NAVAJOS AND APACHES USED CRADLEBOARDS
FOR THEIR YOUNG CHILDREN.

mothers still use cradleboards. A cradleboard is made of three parts: the frame, back slats, and a hoop. The baby is wrapped in layers of cloth and then strapped onto the board. The hoop protects the baby's head in case of a fall. It also is used to support a hood that shields the child's eyes from the sun. The cradleboard makes it easy for the mother to transport the baby, especially when on horseback. In their cradleboards, the babies are less likely to be bothered by snakes and insects.

Babies are generally kept in cradleboards for the first six or seven months of life, until they start to crawl. Newborn infants spend most of their time in their cradleboards. As they grow older, they spend more time out, being held by their mothers or other relatives. Being in a cradleboard tends to flatten the back of a baby's head.

Childhood → As soon as children were old enough, they were expected to help. Their first jobs would include dressing themselves and bringing in firewood. In the traditional way of life, the children would work with the adults in their extended family. The parents, grandparents, aunts, uncles, and cousins who lived nearby made up the extended family. The children would help as they could and learn as they went along.

AN IMPORTANT PART OF AN APACHEAN CHILD-
HOOD WAS LISTENING TO THE LEGENDS AND
STORIES TOLD BY THE ELDERS OF THE COMMUNITY.

As the children learned the skills of everyday life, they were also taught about their culture. The adults told stories to teach the children about history, religion, and correct behavior. Sometimes the stories would deal with real people and events. Other times they would tell about spirits and the supernatural beings that are part of their religion.

In the past there were many important things for the children to learn. Children learned to run fast and ride horses. It was important to be able to escape if enemies attacked. Girls had to learn the many tasks required to provide for the needs of the family. This included learning about plants and their uses. Girls would also learn how to make the many items that the family needed, such as clothes, moccasins, baskets, and other everyday items.

Boys learned to hunt and make their own weapons. The older boys often accompanied the men on hunting and raiding trips but were not allowed to fight. They would help in other ways—taking care of the

NAVAJO SHEPHERDS STOP
AT A WATERING HOLE.

camp, collecting wood, cooking, fetching water, making beds, and tending the horses. The boys would also be in charge of guarding the camp. When they could do all of this well, they were considered adults.

As the children grew, their responsibilities increased. They were expected to do as much as they could to assist their families. Tending the flocks is one responsibility that often falls to Navajo children even today. Every morning the flocks of sheep and goats have to be let out of the corral. Then the animals must be watched while they graze. The flock must be moved constantly to prevent them from eating all the food in one area. The children must also make sure that none of the animals wanders off.

Today Apache and Navajo children are still expected to work with and for the other members of their families. They have to balance traditional responsibilities with the demands of the modern world.

Today Apache and Navajo children attend schools that are just like schools all over the United States. They learn the same subjects, play the same games, read the same books, and have the same vacations. When at home, most are still taught about their culture in the traditional way.

Hunting ➡ Over time the sources of food for the Apaches and Navajos have changed. When they first

LEARNING HOW TO WEAVE
AS WELL AS COOK FRY BREAD,
A TRADITIONAL INDIAN FOOD,
ARE PART OF TODAY'S APACHE
AND NAVAJO UPBRINGING.

came to the Southwest, they were hunters and gatherers. They would travel great distances throughout the Southwest to hunt and gather specific foods.

Many different animals were hunted. The most important was the deer. The other large animals they hunted were antelope, elk, mountain sheep, and mountain goats. Occasionally they would take long trips onto the plains to hunt buffalo. Closer to home they would hunt small game. Wood rats, squirrels, rabbits, turkeys, opossums, and porcupines were all included in the diet of the Apaches and Navajos.

Before the introduction of firearms, the bow and arrow was the main hunting weapon of the Apaches and Navajos. Certain groups of Apaches were known to use poison arrows. To get closer to the game, the hunters sometimes used deer and antelope head masks. Hunting parties usually consisted of one to three male hunters. On longer trips as many as ten hunters would travel together.

One hunting technique that the Apaches and Navajos used is called a surround. This method was used primarily for rabbits and occasionally for antelope. Most of the members of the group—men, women, and children—would participate in a surround. For rabbits the group would form a circle around a large area. Then they would all move toward the center, surrounding any rabbits in the area. As the circle became smaller, the hunters would kill the fleeing rabbits with clubs.

Even today, when most Apaches and Navajos shop at grocery stores for much of their food, hunting is an important part of their culture. Young boys are still taught how to hunt.

Gathering ➤ There was a time when wild plants and animals were the only food available for the Apaches and Navajos. During the spring, summer, and fall, they would travel to different areas to collect various wild plants. Mainly it was the women who did the gathering, but sometimes the men would go along to help and to act as guards. Many different plants were gathered. The most important were the mescal (also called century plant or agave) and piñon nuts.

The mescal plant has a core of leaves that resembles an artichoke heart and is called the head (not the heart) of the mescal. These heads were separated from the plants, baked in rock-lined underground ovens, dried in the sun, and then stored. The finished mescal was similar to squash. The baked and dried mescal heads were sometimes pounded into flat sheets. The sheets could be stored for longer periods of time.

In the fall it was time to gather piñon nuts. The piñon is a pine tree that grows in the Southwest. Piñon nuts grow in the pine cones. Often the whole group would travel to the piñon forests to gather the nuts, which fall to the ground when ripe. Sometimes the people shook the tree limbs to get the nuts to fall. When the nuts were not quite ripe, they would roast the pine cones to get the nuts out.

After the nuts were collected they were roasted, shelled, and ground into flour. The piñon flour was used to make a form of bread and also used in soups. Some nuts were kept in the shell to be eaten whole.

The berries, seeds, and leaves of many other plants were gathered too.

The Apaches and Navajos used each plant to its fullest. They ate a portion of the plants fresh and stored the rest for later use. They devised many ways to store food for the winter.

In the dry Southwest, the sun was the major food preserver. Food to be stored would often be laid out in the sun to dry and then placed in baskets and other storage containers. A dry cave made an excellent storage space. After putting their food in the caves, the Apaches and Navajos would seal the opening with rocks. They then covered the rocks with mud and dirt to conceal the opening. Some of the food would be cached, or hidden, where it was gathered. The people would also carry some of the food with them. During

CORNMEAL WAS TRADITIONALLY USED IN NAVAJO
WEDDING CEREMONIES. IN THIS OLD CUSTOM,
THE BRIDE'S GRANDMOTHER PRESENTED THE COUPLE
WITH A SPECIAL BASKET FILLED WITH CORNMEAL.
THE BRIDE AND GROOM THEN EXCHANGED
PINCHES OF THE CORNMEAL WITH ONE ANOTHER.

the year they would make trips back to the various storage places to pick up food. Stored in this way, food would keep for a long time.

The Apaches and Navajos gathered many plants for use as medicines as well as food. They were accomplished herbalists (people skilled in gathering and using herbs as medicines).

Agriculture ➤ Scientists believe that agriculture in the Americas was first developed in Central America. The Indians there began to grow corn six to eight thousand years ago. By the time Christopher Columbus sailed, corn was the major source of food for many tribes throughout the Americas. The Apaches and Navajos probably learned agriculture from the Puebloan people of the Southwest. The Pueblo Indians were accomplished farmers. Different groups of Apaches and Navajos adopted agriculture to different degrees.

The Navajos became the most accomplished farmers among the Apachean people. The various other Apache groups adopted agriculture less completely than the Navajos. Some groups—Western Apache, Lipan, Chiricahua, and Mescalero—grew corn. Some would set up their summer camps at a good spot to grow corn. Once the corn was planted, often the oldest and youngest members of the band would be left to tend it. The others in the band would travel out from the camp to hunt and gather. The Jicarillas and the Kiowa Apaches adopted a lifestyle closer to the Plains Indians. They depended very little on agriculture.

Types of Crops ➤ Corn was the most important crop. By the time the Spanish arrived, beans and squash were also being grown. Many new crops were introduced by the Spanish. By the time the Southwest became part of the United States, they were growing a wide variety of crops.

Food Preparation ➛ Corn was prepared in many different ways. Sometimes the ears of corn were baked or boiled and eaten fresh. The Apaches used the traditional underground ovens to bake their corn. The Navajos, however, like their Puebloan neighbors, sometimes used a beehive-shaped outdoor oven copied from the Spanish. This type of oven, made of stones and adobe mud, is still used by many Indians in the Southwest.

A fire would be built in the oven and kept going all day. When the fire burned down, the coals and ashes would be raked out. The corn would then be placed in the oven with some water. The oven would be sealed with a large rock and mud. The corn would be left to cook all night until the oven cooled. In the morning the corn would be removed from the oven. The corn kernels were then scraped from the cobs and left in the sun to dry.

After drying, the corn was ready to use immediately or to be stored. To use the corn in cooking, the people often ground it into cornmeal. The cornmeal was used to make many different foods: tortillas, tamales, soups, mushes, and corn cakes.

To make cornmeal, the dried corn was ground with two pieces of stone. The corn kernels were placed on a flat, rectangular stone called the metate. A cylindrical stone called the mano was then held in both hands and moved up and down against the metate to crush the kernels. (*Mano* is the Spanish word for hand.)

Introduction of Livestock ➤ The Apaches and Navajos had a varied and complete diet that included wild plants and animals and the crops they learned to grow. As time went on, many of the groups also began to depend on domesticated animals for food.

With the exception of the dog, there were no domesticated animals native to the Americas. The Spanish brought horses, sheep, cattle, goats, pigs, and other domesticated animals to the Southwest. The Puebloan people quickly added animal husbandry to their farming communities. The Apaches and Navajos adopted these new animals in varying degrees.

The Apaches and Navajos were among the first Indians in North America to get horses. The horse gave the Apaches and Navajos great mobility. This ability to move quickly over great distances allowed them to expand their activities. The horse allowed the

TOP: ALONG WITH CORN, BEANS, SQUASHES, PUMPKIN, AND CHILES PREDOMINATE IN NAVAJO COOKING. BOTTOM: THE NAVAJOS AND APACHES WERE AMONG THE FIRST NORTH AMERICAN INDIANS TO GET HORSES. THIS ENABLED THEM TO TRAVEL GREATER DISTANCES.

Apaches and Navajos to raid their Puebloan and Spanish neighbors. The horse was also a source of food in times of shortage.

In addition to horses the Navajos adopted other domestic animals. They came to depend very heavily on their herds of sheep and goats. The sheep's wool and the goat's mohair were woven into blankets and other textiles. These animals became a primary source of food, clothing, and trade goods. Even today Navajos are often judged by the number and quality of their animals.

As the Navajos became more dependent on their herds and farming, their culture changed. They became less like their Apache cousins. The Apaches maintained a lifestyle closer to their hunting and gathering past while depending on the horse extensively.

Tools, Weapons, and Other Everyday Items ➤ As hunters and gatherers the Apaches and Navajos used many tools and weapons. All of these were made of natural materials. Wood, bones, antlers, and stone were all used to make tools.

The most important weapon of the Apaches and Navajos was the bow and arrow. The Apaches and Navajos introduced a different style of bow to the Southwest. The bows were single-curved self-bows 3 to 4 feet (0.9 to 1.2 m) long. A self-bow is made from one piece of wood. The first choice in wood was mulberry. The Indians also made bows of locust, oak, and maple. The bowstring was made from deer sinew. Sinew is the tissue surrounding muscles. The longest sinews, which are found in the deer's leg, were preferred for bowstrings.

The Apaches and Navajos took pride in their weapons and made decorated bow cases and quivers. The best bow cases and quivers were made from the skins of mountain lions. Mountain lion skins were thought to bring good luck to the hunter.

Arrows were made in two ways. One type was made of a solid piece of hardwood 2 feet (0.6 m) long. The favorite woods were mountain mahogany, Apache plume, and mulberry. The other style of arrow had two parts. The main shaft of the arrow was made from a hollow cane or reed. A hardwood foreshaft was inserted into the main shaft. These arrows were 2½ feet (0.8 m) long.

Both styles of arrows had three split feathers spaced evenly apart. The feathers were attached with wet sinew. The Apaches and Navajos generally did not make arrowheads. Instead they sharpened and then fire-hardened the tips of the arrows. However, they would use stone points for arrowheads when they found them.

Poison arrows were occasionally used for hunting. The arrows were tipped with a variety of poisons, including snake and spider venom and a poison made from the gallbladder of a deer.

The Apaches and Navajos also used shields, spears, and war clubs. Sometimes they fashioned protective leather war shirts and war hats. Young boys made slings which they hunted with. The sling was made from a square of leather. A hole was put in each corner and strings were attached. They also made many other tools for everyday use.

Prior to the coming of the Spanish, the Apaches and Navajos used knives made of stone. Both flint and chert were used to make single-edged pointed knives. Sometimes the knives were attached to wooden handles. Leather sheaths were common. After the arrival of the Spanish, the Apaches and Navajos traded for metal knives and other tools.

Firearms quickly became important to the Apaches and Navajos. They would trade for them when they could. Often their raids were aimed at acquiring firearms and ammunition. Some Apaches went as far as making bullets out of silver or rocks when they couldn't get regular bullets.

In addition to their weapons, the Apaches and Navajos had to make many other items that they needed. They were accomplished leatherworkers. They made parfleches (leather storage bags), rope, and clothes using leather. After they acquired horses, they learned how to make saddles and other tack (stable gear).

Even simple items like spoons and ladles had to be made. Dried gourds would be used for ladles and cups. Spoons and dishes would be carved from wood. They made pottery as well.

Shelter ➡ The Apaches and Navajos built a number of different types of housing. The groups that moved frequently needed shelters that could be constructed easily and quickly. The Apache camps were called rancherías.

The Mescalero and the Jicarilla Apaches generally used tipis. These were similar to the tipis used by the Plains Indians. The frame for the tipi was made of poles, which were then covered with hides. The door of the tipi faced east.

The Apaches who lived in the high country built wickiups. A wickiup is constructed by placing slender willow or oak poles in a circle. The poles would then be bent toward the center and tied together. The frame would be about 8 feet (2.5 m) in diameter and 7 feet (2 m) high at the center. Yucca leaves would be used to tie the poles together. The frame would then be covered with grass, brush, or whatever suitable plants were available. The door was covered with a hide. A

THE APACHEAN PEOPLE HAD SEVERAL DIFFERENT KINDS OF HOUSES. THE APACHE WICKIUP (TOP) IS STILL IN USE TODAY IN SOME PLACES. THE HOGAN (BOTTOM) WAS THE PRIMARY SHELTER OF THE NAVAJOS. SOME CEREMONIES, LIKE THE HEALING SING, HAD TO TAKE PLACE IN A HOGAN.

smoke hole was left in the top directly above the central firepit. On occasion wickiups are still used today.

The main shelter of the Navajos is the hogan. The design of the hogan is said to have been a gift from Hastseyalti, the Talking God. Over time the hogan has changed. Originally it was a structure consisting of a circular hole in the ground with a roof of logs covered with earth. For the last 150 years the hogan has primarily been constructed of logs. The logs are stacked to make a six- or eight-sided structure. The roof is made of logs. A log comes up from each corner to the center of the roof. Smaller logs are then placed across the support logs. The logs of the roof and sides were chinked with cedar bark and mud. The roof would then be finished with a thick layer of mud. Some hogans have stone walls.

The door of the hogan faces east, toward the sunrise. The door would be covered with a blanket. At first the door blanket was woven from yucca stalks. A firepit was placed in the center of the hogan and a smoke hole was left above it. Hogans vary in size. Many are about 25 feet (7.5 m) across. Some that are used for special ceremonies are as big as 50 feet (15 m) across. Each new hogan is blessed with a special ceremony. Certain activities of the Navajos can only take place within a hogan. Today many Navajos still live in hogans. They are a Navajo tradition.

The hogan has many advantages as a home. It is easily heated in the winter. It stays cool in the summer. It provides protection against the strong spring winds of the Southwest.

Another structure that was used by both the Apaches and Navajos is the ramada, or shade house. The ramada consists of four upright poles supporting a roof of brush. Sometimes brush walls would be added to one or more sides. The ramada provided the Apaches and Navajos with a cool, shaded area in which to work in the summer. Ramadas are still used.

THE NAVAJOS AND APACHES ALSO USED A RAMADA, OR SHADE HOUSE. THIS STRUCTURE WAS A RELIEF FROM THE HOT SUN IN THE SUMMER.

A HOGAN IS IN THE BACK-GROUND.

A NAVAJO
BUCKSKIN SUIT
WITH BEAUTIFUL
BEADING

Clothing ➤ The earliest form of dress among the Apaches and Navajos probably consisted of a simple skirt made from the hides of deer, elk, antelope, or buffalo. Robes were worn as needed for protection against the weather. The people wore hard-soled moccasins on their feet. Some believe that the Apaches and Navajos were the first to bring this type of footwear to the Southwest.

As time went on, they made more elaborate clothing from buckskin. Women began to wear buckskin shirts and skirts, which were sometimes decorated with fringe. The men would wear a buckskin loincloth that hung down to the knees in front and to the ankles in back. In the warm months the men did not wear a top. In the winter they wore long-sleeve buckskin shirts. The men's shirts were also decorated with fringe on the shoulders and sleeves. The children wore little or nothing in the summer. In the colder months they dressed like the adults.

Knee-high or taller moccasins completed the outfit. The tops of the moccasins would be folded down. A knife or other small object was often kept in the folds.

The early Apache and Navajo men wore their hair loose. They used a headband to keep their hair out of their faces. Often the women wore their hair parted, drawn back, and knotted in shape like an hourglass.

Navajo dress began to be influenced by the Puebloan style. The women began to wear mantas, a woolen dress, and high buckskin leggings. Many of the men continued to wear buckskin, although some began to adopt the Pueblo style of pants. The Navajos also used the Puebloan hairstyle. They pulled their hair back and wrapped and tied it.

Navajo clothing styles for women changed while the Navajos were being held at Fort Sumner. During this time Navajo clothing was influenced by the styles of the soldiers' wives. The Navajo women began wearing velveteen blouses and cotton skirts. Many "traditional" Navajo women still wear them.

CRAFTS

The Apaches and Navajos are accomplished craftspeople. Today their crafts are highly valued and known throughout the world. Basketmaking, weaving, and silversmithing are the best-known products of the Apache and Navajo craftsmen. The Apaches and Navajos also make pottery for everyday use.

Basketmaking ➜ Basketmaking is most important among the Apaches. No one knows for sure how or when the Apaches learned to make baskets. Basketmaking is a complex process. It was done exclusively by the Apache women. The materials for the baskets would be collected in the winter when the fibers were easier to dry. A wide variety of fibers was used. The

THE BEAUTY AND GRACE OF THESE
APACHE BASKETS ARE EXCEPTIONAL.

yucca plant alone could provide three or four different fibers and colors. Other fibers were taken from such plants as the willow, sumac, mulberry, unicorn plant, cottonwood, and devil's-weed.

One of the most common Apache baskets was the Apache water jug, called the *tus.* To make a *tus,* the women first made an open wicker jug. The jug was then lined with the pitch of the piñon pine to make it waterproof. Sometimes the pitch was put on the outside of the *tus* as well. Although men were allowed to watch the weaving of the *tus,* the women sealed the jug with pitch secretly.

The Apaches made many other types of baskets. Each type had its special use. The *tuts-ah,* or burden basket, was a larger version of the *tus.* It was not lined because it was not used for carrying water. The *tuts-ah* was used for carrying heavy loads when the Apaches gathered firewood and plants. The *tsah,* a shallow tray, was the most widely used Apache basket. It was fashioned from coils of fiber and had many uses.

Weaving → Who originally taught the Navajos to weave is open to debate. The Navajos claim to have learned the skill from Spider Woman, one of their supernatural beings. Many archaeologists believe that the Navajos learned weaving from the Pueblo Indians. Either way, it was not until they acquired their own herds of sheep and goats that weaving became important.

Among the Navajos, weaving is an activity done almost exclusively by women. Girls start helping sometimes when they are as young as three or four years old.

The Navajos use a rigid-frame upright loom made of wood. Their blankets and rugs have a continuous warp, the long vertical yarn onto which the pattern is woven. Three types of blankets and rugs are woven. They are regular weave; double weave, or twill; and two-faced, or double-sided, weaving. Regular weave has the same pattern on both sides. Double weave, or twill, has a design on one side and the reversed pattern on the other side. Double-sided weaving has different patterns on each side.

Yarn to be woven is either left in its natural colors or dyed with vegetable dyes or aniline dyes. For natural colors, different colors of wool and mohair are spun separately. Vegetable dyes are dyes made from plants, roots, or bark. Aniline dyes are chemical dyes that were introduced first by the Spanish and later by Anglo traders.

There are many steps involved in creating a blanket or rug. Each spring the sheep and goats need to be shorn. The wool and mohair that is clipped off the sheep and goats, respectively, is very dirty and must be cleaned. Next, it is carded. Carding is done with two instruments called cards. Each card looks like a rectangular Ping-Pong paddle covered with small hooks. As the wool and mohair is carded, all the individual hairs are drawn out. This helps make sure the hairs are lying in the same direction. After the wool is carded, it is spun.

Spinning the hair creates the yarn to be used in the weaving. The spindle is the most important Na-

THIS NAVAJO WOMAN
IS WEAVING A RUG
INSIDE A HOGAN.

THE COLORS IN THE
NAVAJO BLANKET
ARE MADE FROM
EITHER VEGETABLE
OR CHEMICAL DYE.

vajo spinning tool. A spindle looks like a large toy top. The spindle is spun by twirling it. The yarn is respun a number of times. Each time the yarn gets finer. After the spinning is completed, the yarn is dyed the various colors needed for the rug. No dyeing is needed if the rug is to be woven using natural colors.

The next steps are to set up the loom and begin the weaving. For a vegetable-dyed rug of 3 feet by 5 feet (0.9 m by 1.5 m), it takes close to four hundred hours of work to go from shearing the sheep to finished rug.

Over time the Navajos have developed regional styles of weaving. Someone who is familiar with Navajo weaving can often tell where on the reservation a rug was made.

Silversmithing ➤ Long before the arrival of the white man, the Puebloan people of the Southwest were making jewelry from turquoise and other colorful stones. Silversmithing, however, was not known until it was brought to the Southwest by the Spanish. Spaniards used silverwork decoratively on their clothes and horses. Today, silver, turquoise, and other colorful stones and shells are combined to create beautiful jewelry.

Among the Navajos, silversmithing was not known until the 1850s. The early silversmiths fashioned simple ornaments using melted-down or hammered silver coins. Around 1880 the Navajo silversmiths added turquoise to their silverwork.

Today there are many talented Navajo silversmiths. Their work is known and appreciated throughout the world.

BEAUTIFUL SILVER
AND TURQUOISE JEWELRY
MADE BY THE NAVAJOS
IS IN GREAT DEMAND.

APACHES AND NAVAJOS TODAY

Most Apaches and Navajos still live on reservations. There are approximately two hundred thousand Apaches and Navajos living on reservations in the Southwest. Farming and ranching are still important activities. In addition, tourism, craftwork, and timber and other natural-resource management all play a part in supporting the tribes today.

Almost all Apache and Navajo children attend school today. Many go on to colleges and universities. At the same time, many tribal members still live without modern conveniences. They prefer to live a more traditional lifestyle. One of the difficulties of growing up an American Indian today is trying to balance the traditional view of the world with that of mainstream America.

NAVAJOS WHO LIVE
ON RESERVATIONS TODAY
STILL HOLD TRIBAL
MEETINGS TO DISCUSS
COMMUNITY BUSINESS.

ALTHOUGH MANY
APACHES AND NAVAJOS
HAVE LEFT THE
RESERVATION, OTHERS
LIVE AND WORK THERE.

THIS NAVAJO WOMAN
WORKS IN THE
POST OFFICE ON A
NAVAJO RESERVATION.

FOR FURTHER READING

Bahti, Tom. *Southwestern Indian Ceremonials*. Las Vegas, Nev.: KC Publications, 1970.

———. *Southwestern Indian Tribes*. Las Vegas, Nev.: KC Publications, 1968.

Bailey, Garrick, and Robert Glenn Bailey. *A History of the Navajo: The Reservation Years*. Santa Fe, N. Mex.: School of American Research Press, 1986.

Baldwin, Gordon C. *The Apache Indians, Raiders of the Southwest*. New York: Four Winds Press, 1978.

Dutton, Bertha P. *American Indians of the Southwest*. Albuquerque: University of New Mexico Press, 1983.

Erdoes, Richard. *The Native Americans: Navajos*. New York: Sterling Publishing, 1978.

Haley, James L. *Apaches: A History and Culture Portrait*. Garden City, N.Y.: Doubleday, 1981.

Loh, Jules. *Lords of the Earth: A History of the Navajo Indians*. New York: Crowell-Collier, 1971.

McKissack, Patricia. *The Apache*. Chicago: Children's Press, 1984.

Niethammer, Carolyn. *American Indian Food and Lore*. New York: Colliers, 1974.

Robinson, Maudie. *Children of the Sun: The Pueblos, Navajos and Apaches of New Mexico*. New York: Julian Messner, 1973.

INDEX